THE SINKING OF THE SS TITANIC

April 14-15, 1912

By Jack Thayer

Spitfire Publishers

First published privately in a limited run of 500 hardback copies by the author in 1940. This paperback edition published by Spitfire Publishers Ltd in 2019.

In memory of John Borland Thayer 1862-1912

CONTENTS

ABOUT 'THE SINKING OF THE SS TITANIC'

On 14 April 1912, John B. 'Jack' Thayer III, the 17-year-old heir to a Pennsylvania railroad fortune, was traveling first class with his mother, father and their maid on the most spectacular ship of the era – the *Titanic*.

Jack was one of only a handful of survivors who escaped by jumping into the freezing Atlantic as the *Titanic* sank and spent the next five hours clinging onto collapsible lifeboat B, the last lifeboat swept off the ship's boat deck. He barely survived the disaster, and his detailed and shocking account of that fateful night riveted those he recounted it to in the following decades. Finally, in 1940, he wrote down what happened for his family, privately printing 500 copies. Five years later, after the tragic loss of his son in the Second World War, Jack Thayer committed suicide, and his story was mostly forgotten.

This new edition published in 2019 includes the historically important series of six drawings by

Lewis Skidmore a young art teacher aboard the *Carpathia*, the liner that came to the aid of the *Titanic* survivors. Jack described to Lewis the stages of the *Titanic's* demise, which Skidmore faithfully drew. Critically it shows the ship breaking in two as she sank. Many survivors refuted this assessment but seventy years later Jack was proved correct when the wreck was discovered resting on the seabed – in two halves. This edition also includes further bonus material, Jack's earlier, much shorter accounts of his amazing escape published in 1912 and 1913.

About the Author

John 'Jack' B. Thayer III, was born in Philadelphia on 24 December 1894 into the wealthy and aristocratic Thayer family. His father was John Thayer II who ran the Pennsylvania Railroad Company, his mother, socialite Marian Thayer. After surviving the disaster he graduated from the University of Pennsylvania, served as an artillery officer in the First World War, went into banking and was later financial vice president of the University of Pennsylvania. He committed suicide on September 20, 1945 following several years of depression, he was found in a car in Philadelphia his throat and wrists cut. He was survived by his wife Lois Cassatt, son John, and three daughters, Lois, Julie and Pauline.

Praise for 'The Sinking of the SS Titanic'

'A vivid account of how the *Titanic* sank by survivor Jack Thayer' *The Daily Telegraph*

'A dramatic first-hand account... *Titanic* survivor reveals the horrifying cries of the luxury liner's dying victims' *The Daily Mail*

PREFACE

This account of the sinking of the SS *Titanic* has I been written primarily as a family record for the information of my children and perhaps their children in memory of my father, John Borland Thayer, the third of that name, who lost his life in the disaster.

Just as no two happenings in the stream of space time are identical, no two ships either destroyed by an 'act of God' in peace time, or of an 'enemy' in time of war, sink in the same manner or under the same conditions. And due to the great size of modern ships no two individuals no matter how close they may be together on shipboard have the same description of experience to relate, should they be so fortunate as to survive the ordeal. Therefore, every account by an individual survivor of such a disaster probably has some new reader interest to those interested in stories of the sea.

It takes the many separate accounts pieced together to give the true composite history of the whole happening and I hope this attempt at a true description of the *Titanic* disaster may have some historical value.

The ship was carrying 2,208 persons. Seven hundred and three persons left the ship in the lifeboats, leaving 1,553 to go down with the ship. Forty-two of these were saved; 28 were on the bottom of an overturned lifeboat, and of this number I was one; and fourteen were in the half submerged collapsible boat, among whom was my good friend Richard Norris Williams, who also lost his father. Only about one in every thirty-six who went down with the ship was saved, and I happened to be one of those.

The whole event passes before me now in 1940, as vividly and with the same clarity, as twenty-eight years ago in 1912. Nevertheless, in writing this story I have referred to statistics and a brief article prepared by me shortly after the disaster.

I want to emphasize some of the everyday conditions under which we were then living, to show how much humanity was shocked by the approaching disaster.

These were ordinary days, and into them had crept only gradually the telephone, the talking machine, the automobile. The airplane due to have so soon such a stimulating yet devastating effect on civilization, was only a few years old, and the radio as known today, was still in the scientific laboratory. The Marconi wireless had just come into commercial use, and the Morse code for help was CQD, as our modern SOS was just making its appearance. The safety razor had just been invented, and its use was gradually spreading. Upon rising in the morning, we looked forward to a normal day of customary business progress. The conservative morning paper seldom had headlines larger than half an inch in height. Upon reaching the breakfast table, our perusal of the morning paper was slow and deliberate. We did not nervously clutch for it, and rapidly scan the glaring headlines, as we are inclined to do today. Nothing was revealed in the morning, the trend of which was not known the night before. We knew that our morning coffee came from Brazil; that it was grown as a free crop, without destruction of the surplus; that it was purchased from the small corner grocer, a friend, at a price established by competition, without the loading and build-up, due to many hidden taxes; and that it was not 'dated.' These days were peaceful and ruled by economic theory and practice built up over years of slow and hardly perceptible change. There was peace, and the world had an even tenor to its ways.

A dollar could be exchanged for four shillings, four marks, or five francs. In exchange for a five-dollar gold piece or a five-dollar bill, one could pocket a pound note or a gold sovereign.

As an individual, returning to Haverford School outside of Philadelphia, I confidently knew that after graduation in the Spring, and according to plans for my future laid down by my father in deference to my nebulous ambitions, I would attend college at Princeton, New Jersey, and from there go to London, Paris, Berlin, and Vienna, where I would serve an apprenticeship in private and commercial banking houses, and would return to practice commercial or private banking in the United States. It could be planned. It was planned. It was a certainty.

In those days one could freely circulate around the world, in both a physical and an economic sense, and definitely plan for the future, unhampered by class, nationality, or government.

True enough, from time to time there were events – catastrophes – like the Johnstown flood, the San Francisco earthquake, or floods in China – which stirred the sleeping world, but not enough to keep it from resuming its slumber. It seems to me that the disaster about to occur was the event, which not only made the world rub its eyes and awake, but woke it with a start, keeping it moving at a rapidly accelerating pace ever since, with less and less peace, satisfaction, and happiness.

Today the individual has to be contented with rapidity of motion, nervous emotion, and economic insecurity. To my mind the world of today awoke April 15th, 1912.

THE SINKING OF THE SS TITANIC APRIL 14-15, 1912

The SS *Titanic* of the White Star Line, largest ship the world had ever known, sailed from Southampton on her maiden voyage to New York, on April 10, 1912. She was built by Messrs Harland and Wolff, at Belfast. She was a fabricated steel vessel of gigantic dimensions, registered at Liverpool, her gross tonnage was 46,328 tons, her length overall being 852 feet, with a breadth of 92 feet and a depth of 65 feet. The distance from the keel to the top of the funnels was 175 feet. She had a double bottom extending the full length of the ship, with a space five to six feet between the inner and outer plates, and was divided into sixteen water-tight compartments, with access to each compartment through water-tight doors. The rudder alone weighed 100 tons. She was driven by three enormous screws, the center one weighing 22 tons, the other two 38 tons each, and was capable of making 23 knots. The last word in luxury, she was thought unsinkable.

Captain E. J. Smith, her commander, commodore of the White Star Line fleet, was on his last round trip from Southampton, before having to retire on age. In his 38 years of service he had never met with a serious accident. On this trip he had under him a splendid complement of officers and men.

The *Titanic* had a passenger certificate to carry 3,547 passengers and crew. She carried sixteen lifeboats and four Engelhart collapsible boats, all of which had a total carrying capacity of 1,167 persons, or approximately 60 to 65 in each boat. She carried 3,560 lifebelts or their equivalent.

The *Titanic* was a wonderfully safe vessel. The lifes-saving equipment should surely have been sufficient to take care of any normal eventualities.

On this maiden voyage the ship carried a total of 2,208 persons, of whom 1,316 were passengers and 892 crew. There were 332 first-class passengers, 277 second-class passengers and 709 third-class passengers. I have in my safe deposit box an original first-class passenger list. It was carried off the ship in the pocket of the overcoat worn by my mother.

There were a great many prominent people on the passenger list and because it was her maiden voyage there were on board many of those responsible for the building of the ship and the management of the steamship line. Some of these were: Thomas Andrews, one of the ship's designers; Archie Frost, the builders' chief engineer, including his approximately twenty assistants; J. Bruce Ismay, president of the International Mercantile Marine Company and chairman of the board and managing director of the Oceanic Steam Navigation Company, Limited, owners of the White Star Line; all observing the performance of the ship, and all of whom were often with my father and myself, during the few days we were aboard the ship.

My father, John B. Thayer, second vice-president of the Pennsylvania Railroad, my mother, Marian Longstreth Morris Thayer, my mother's maid, Margaret Fleming, and I were all in one party that sailed first-class from Southampton.

We had no more than started down the narrow channel, and were commencing to make headway under our own power, when we passed the American Liner SS *St Paul*, tied up to the SS *Oceanic* which was lying alongside the dock. The suction created by our port propeller, as we made a turn in the narrow channel, broke the strong cables mooring her to the *Oceanic* causing her stern to swing toward us at a rapid rate. It looked as though there would surely be a collision. Her stern could not have been more than a yard or two from our side. It almost hit us. Luckily, the combined effort of several tugs, which had quickly made fast to her, pulled her stern back. This narrowly averted collision was considered an ill-omen by all those accustomed to the sea.

We called at Cherbourg, and from there proceeded to Queenstown.

We left Queenstown at 1.30 in the afternoon of Thursday, April 11. The weather was fair and clear, the ship palatial, the food delicious. Almost everyone was counting the days till we would see the Statue of Liberty.

I occupied a stateroom adjoining that of my father and mother on the port side of 'C' deck; and, needless to say, being seventeen years old, I was all over the ship.

Sunday, April 14th, dawned bright and clear. It looked as if we were in for another very pleasant day. I spent most of that day walking around the decks with my mother and father. We had short chats with many of the other promenaders, among whom I particularly remember J. Bruce Ismay, Thomas Andrews, and Charles M. Hays, who was president of the Grand Trunk Railway of Canada; with all of whom we spent quite a lot of time.

It became noticeably colder as the afternoon wore on. I remember Mr Ismay showing us a wire regarding the presence of ice and remarking that we would not reach that position until around 9 pm. We went to our staterooms about 6.30 to dress for dinner. My father and mother were invited out to dinner that night, so I dined alone at our regular table. After dinner I was enjoying a cup of coffee, when a man about 28 or 30 years of age drew up, and introduced himself as Milton C. Long, son of Judge Charles M. Long, of Springfield, Massachusetts. He was travelling alone. We talked together for an hour or so. Afterwards I put on an overcoat and took a few turns around the deck.

It had become very much colder. It was a brilliant, starry night. There was no moon and I have never seen the stars shine brighter; they appeared to stand right out of the sky, sparkling like cut diamonds. A very light haze, hardly noticeable, hung low over the water. I have spent much time on the ocean, yet I have never seen the sea smoother than it was that night; it was like a mill pond, and just as innocent looking, as the great ship quietly rippled through it. I went onto the boat deck – it was deserted and lonely. The wind whistled through the stays, and blackish smoke poured out of the three forward funnels; the fourth funnel was a dummy for ventilation purposes. It was the kind of a night that made one feel glad to be alive.

About eleven o'clock I went below to my stateroom. After a short conversation with my father and mother, and saying good night to them, I stepped into my room to put on pyjamas expecting to have another delightful night's rest like the four preceding.

The ship was so large and extensive that all I can tell about the tragedy is only a small part of all that actually occurred. I will try to recount all that I actually saw or heard, or heard from others and afterwards verified.

We were steaming along a 22 or 23 knots, not reducing speed at all, in spite of the many warnings of the presence of ice, which had come in from other ships during the afternoon and evening. We were out for a record run.

I had called 'goodnight' to my father and mother

in the next room. In order to get plenty of air, I had half opened the port, and the breeze was coming through with a quiet humming whistle.

There was the steady rhythmic pulsation of the engines and screws, the feel and hearing of which becomes second nature to one, after a few hours at sea. It was a fine night for sleeping, and with the day's air and exercise, I was sleepy.

I wound my watch – it was 11.45 pm – and was just about to step into bed, when I seemed to sway slightly. I immediately realized that the ship had veered to port as though she had been gently pushed. If I had had brimful glass of water in my hand not a drop would have been spilled, the shock was so slight.

Almost instantaneously the engines stopped. The sudden quiet was startling and disturbing. Like the subdued quiet in a sleeping car, at a stop, after a continuous run. Not a sound except the breeze whistling through the half open port. Then there was the distant noise of running feet and muffled voices, as several people hurried through the passageway. Very shortly the engines started up again – slowly – not with the bright vibration to which we were accustomed, but as though they were tired. After very few revolutions they again stopped.

I hurried into my heavy overcoat and drew on my slippers. All excited, but not thinking anything serious had occurred, I called in to my father and mother that 'I was going up on deck to see the fun.' Father said he would put on his clothes and come right up and join me. It was bitterly cold. I walked around the deck looking over the side from time to time. As far as I could see, there was nothing to be seen, except something scattered on the well deck forward, which I afterwards learned was ice. There was no sign of any large iceberg. Only two or three people were on deck when I arrived, but many rapidly gathered. My father joined me very soon. He and I moved around the deck trying to discover what had happened and finally found one of the crew who told us we had hit an iceberg, which he tried to point out to us, but which we could not see in spite of the brilliant night, as possibly our eyes were not accustomed to the dark after coming out of the lighted ship.

The ship took on a very slight list to starboard. We did not know it at the moment, but we learned afterward that the iceberg had ripped open probably four of her larger forward compartments on the starboard side; and also that if we had only hit the ice head on, instead of making too late an attempt to avoid it, the ship would in all probability have survived the collision.

About fifteen minutes after the collision, she developed a list to port and was distinctly down by the head.

Here we were 800 miles out from New York, off the Grand Banks, our position latitude 41 degrees, 46 minutes north, longitude 50 degrees, 14 minutes west. No one yet thought of any serious trouble. The ship was unsinkable.

It was now shortly after midnight. My father and I came in from the cold deck to the hallway or lounge. There were quite a few people standing around questioning each other in a dazed kind of way. No one seemed to know what next to do. We saw, as they passed, Mr Ismay, Mr Andrews and some of the ship's officers. Mr Andrews told us he did not give the ship much over an hour to live. We could hardly believe it, and yet if he said so, it must be true. No one was better qualified to know.

I was still just dressed in pyjamas and overcoat. At about 12.15 am the stewards passed the word around for everyone to get fully clothed and put on life preservers, which were in each stateroom. We went below right away and found my mother and her maid fully dressed. I hurried into my clothes – a warm greenish tweed suit and vest with another mohair vest underneath my coat. We all tied on life preservers, which were really large thick cork vests. On top of these we put our overcoats.

We then hurried up to the lounge on 'A' deck, which was now crowded with people, some standing, some hurrying, some pushing out onto the deck. My friend Milton Long came by at the time and asked if he could stay with us. There was a great deal of noise. The band was playing lively tunes without apparently receiving much attention from the worried moving audience.

It has been more or less definitively established by the investigations into the disaster, held both in the United States and in England, that the SS *Cali-*

fornian passed the SS *Titanic* at about 12.30 am, and did see the distress rockets which were continually sent up. She must have seen our blinker light CQD, which was continuously operating. It was determined that her wireless operator signed off after talking to the *Titanic* at about 11.30 pm but possibly even heard our wireless CQD. The captain apparently paid no attention to any reports from his juniors. While I did not see the masthead lights of the SS *Californian* many claim they did see them. My mother watched them for some time while on the port side, waiting to get into a lifeboat, and Second Officer Lightoller told me he positively saw them. The ship was at the most not more than ten or twelve miles away. By merely obeying the age old law of the sea, the captain of the ship had the greatest opportunity ever presented to save over 1,500 human lives with the minimum of effort or danger to his own ship.

We all went out onto 'A' deck, trying to find where we were supposed to go. They were then uncovering the boats and making preparations to swing them out. Everything was fairly orderly, and the crew at least seemed to know what they were doing.

It was now about 12.45 am. The noise was terrific. The deep vibrating roar of the exhaust steam blowing off through the safety valves was deafening, in addition to which they had commenced to send up rockets. There was more and more action. After standing there for some minutes, talking above the din, trying to determine what we should do next, we finally decided to go back into the crowded hallway where it was warm. Shortly we heard the stewards passing the word around: 'all women to the port side.' We then said goodbye to my mother at the head of the stairs on 'A' deck and she and the maid went out onto the port side of that deck, supposedly to get into a lifeboat. Father and I went out on the starboard side, watching what was going on about us. It seemed we were always waiting for orders and no orders ever came. No one knew his boat position, as no lifeboat drill had been held. The men had not yet commenced to lower any of the forward starboard lifeboats, of which there were four. The noise kept up. The deck seemed to be well lighted. People like ourselves were just standing around, out of the way. The stokers, dining-room stewards, and some others of the crew were lined up, waiting for orders. The second and third-class passengers were pouring up onto the deck from the stern, augmenting the already large crowd.

Finally we thought we had better inquire whether or not mother had been able to get a boat. We went into the hall and happened to meet the chief dining-room steward. He told us that he had just seen my mother, and that she had not yet been put into a boat. We found her, and were told that they were loading the forward boats on the port side from the deck below. The ship had a substantial list to port, which made quite a space between the side of the ship and the lifeboats, swinging out over the water, so the crew stretched folded steamer chairs across the space, over which the people were helped into the boats.

We proceeded to the deck below. Father, mother and the maid, went ahead of Long and myself. The lounge on 'B' deck was filled with a milling crowd, and as we went through the doorway out onto the deck, people pushed between my father and mother and Long and me. Long and I could not catch up and were entirely separated from them. I never saw my father again.

We looked for them, following along to where the port boats were being loaded, but could see nothing of either father or mother. Fully believing that they had both been successful in getting into a boat, Long and I went back through the lounge to the starboard side, thinking of what we should do, and not looking further for my father at all.

It must now have been about 1.25 am. The ship was way down by the head with water entirely covering her bow. She gradually came out of her list to port, and if anything, had a slight list to starboard. The crew had commenced to load and lower the forward starboard boats. These could hold over 60 people, but the officers were afraid to load them to capacity, while suspended by falls, bow and stern, 60 feet over the water. They might have buckled or broken from the falls.

The stern lifeboats, four on the port and four on the starboard side, had already left the ship. One of the first boats to leave carried only twelve people, Sir Cosmo and Lady Duff Gordon, and ten others.

Most of the boats were loaded with about 40 to 45, with the exception of the last few to go, which were loaded to full capacity.

One could see the boats that had already left the ship, standing off about 500 or 600 yards. Apparently there was only one light, about which most of them congregated. They were plainly visible and looked very safe on that calm sea.

On deck, the exhaust steam was still roaring. The lights were still strong. The band, with life preservers on, was still playing. The crowd was fairly orderly. Our own situation was too pressing, the scene too kaleidoscopic for me to retain any detailed picture of individual behaviour. I did see one man come through the door out onto the deck with a full bottle of Gordon's gin. He put it to his mouth and practically drained it. If ever I get out of this alive, I thought, there is one man I will never see again. He apparently fought his way into one of the last two boats, for he was one of the first men I recognized upon reaching the deck of the SS *Carpathia*. Someone told me afterwards that he was a state senator or congressman from Virginia or West Virginia.

There was some disturbance in loading the last two forward starboard boats. A large crowd of men was pressing to get into them. No women were around as far as I could see. I saw Ismay, who had been assisting in the loading of the last boat, push his way into it. It was really every man for himself. Many of the crew and men from the stokehole were lined up, with apparently not a thought of attempting to get into a boat without orders. Purser H. W. McElroy, as brave and as fine a man as ever lived, was standing up in the next to last boat, loading it. Two men, I think they were dining-room stewards, dropped into the boat from the deck above. As they jumped, he fired twice into the air. I do not believe they were hit, but they were quickly thrown out. McElroy did not take a boat and was not saved. I should say that all this took place on 'A' deck, just under the boat deck.

Long and I debated whether or not we should fight our way into one of the last two boats. We could almost see the ship slowly going down by the head. There was so much confusion, we did not think they would reach the water right side up, and decided not to attempt it. I do not know what I thought could happen, but we had not given up hope.

We leaned over the side to watch the next to last boat being lowered. It was terrible. Apparently, for some seconds, there was no one above directing the lowering of the bow and stern falls so that she might be held level. The bow was lowered so fast that the people were almost dumped out into the water. I think, if Long and I, and others, had not yelled up – 'Hold the bow,' they all would have been spilled out. Finally, in a few minutes, she reached the water safely.

ILLUSTRATION SECTION

1. 1912 photograph of collapsible lifeboat B that Jack Thayer was saved by, discovered adrift in the Atlantic by crew from Mackay-Bennett the ship sent to recover bodies of the Titanic's victims.

STRIKES STARBOARD BOW -12 f' Aft

11 45 P.M.

2. Titanic strikes the iceberg 11.45 p.m. First in a series of six sketches drawn on board Carpathia on 15 April by Lewis Skidmore (a young art teacher), based on conversations with Jack Thayer following his rescue. The sketches were first published in American newspapers in 1912 and by 1940 when Jack published this book some of the timings attributed to the drawings were proved a little inaccurate.

SETTLES BY HEAD - BOATS ORDERED OUT   12°⁵ A.M

3. 'Titanic settles by head, boats ordered out.'

SETTLES TO FORWARD STACK
BREAKS BETWEEN STACKS

— 1A0 A.M.

4. 'Titanic settles to forward stack, breaks between stacks'. Jack is one of only a handful of survivors to describe the ship breaking in two as she sank. Many survivors refuted this assessment but seventy years later Jack and others was proved right when the wreck was discovered resting on the seabed in two halves.

5. 'Titanic's forward end floats then sinks'.

6. 'Stern section of Titanic pivots and swings over spot where forward section sank'.

7. 'Final position in which Titanic stayed for several minutes before the final plunge'.

It must now have been about 1.50 am, and, as far as we knew, the last boat had gone. We were not aware of the fact that Second Officer Charles Herbert Lightoller and some of the crew were working desperately on top of one of the deck houses to free and launch one of the four Engelhart collapsible lifeboats. These boats had strong wooden bottoms with sides which could be raised, and all around the hull ran a canvas-covered cork fender with a curved surface.

I argued with Long about our chances. I wanted to jump out and catch the empty lifeboat falls, which were swinging free all the way to the water's edge, with the idea of sliding down and swimming out to the partially filled boats lying off in the distance, for I could swim well. In this way we would be away from the crowd, and away from the suction of the ship when she finally went down. We were still 50 or 60 feet above the water. We could not just jump, for we might hit wreckage or a steamer chair and be knocked unconscious. He argued against it and dissuaded me from doing so. Thank heaven he did. The temperature of the water was 28 degrees Fahrenheit. Four degrees below freezing.

We then went up a sheltered stairway onto the starboard side of the boat deck. There were crowds of people up there. They all seemed to keep as far as possible from the ship's rail. We stood there talking from about 2 am on. We sent messages through each other to our families. At times we were just thoughtful and quiet, but the noise around us did not stop.

So many thoughts passed so quickly through my mind! I thought of all the good times I had had, and of all the future pleasures I would never enjoy; of my father and mother; of my sisters and brother. I looked at myself as though from some far-off place. I sincerely pitied myself. It seemed so unnecessary, but we still had a chance, if only we could keep away from the crowd and the suction of the sinking ship.

I only wish I had kept on looking for my father. I should have realized that he would not have taken a boat, leaving me behind. I afterwards heard from my friend, Richard Norris Williams, the tennis player, that his father and mine were standing in a group consisting of Mr George D. Widener and his son Harry, together with some others. They were close in under the second funnel, which was very near to where Long and I were.

It was now about 2.15 am. We could see the water creeping up the deck, as the ship was going down by the head at a pretty fast rate. The water was right up to the bridge. There must have been over 60 feet of it on top of the bow. As the water gained headway along the deck, the crowd gradually moved with it, always pushing, toward the floating stern and keeping in from the rail of the ship as far as they could. We were a mass of hopeless, dazed humanity, attempting, as the almighty and nature made us, to keep our final breath until the last possible moment. The roaring of the exhaust steam suddenly stopped, making a great quietness, in spite of many mixed noises of hurrying human effort and anguish. As I recall it, the lights were still on, even then. There seemed to be quite a ruddy glare, but it was a murky light, with distant people and objects vaguely outlined. The stars were brilliant and the water oily.

Occasionally there had been a muffled thud or deadened explosion within the ship. Now, without warning she seemed to start forward, moving forward and into the water at an angle of about fifteen degrees. This movement, with the water rushing up toward us was accompanied by a rumbling roar, mixed with more muffled explosions. It was like standing under a steel railway bridge while an express train passes overhead, mingled with the noise of a pressed steel factory and wholesale breakage of china.

Long and I had been standing by the starboard rail, about abreast of the second funnel. Our main thought was to keep away from the crowd and the suction. At the rail we were entirely free of the crowd. We had previously decided to jump into the water before she actually went down, so that we might swim some distance away, and avoid what we thought would be terrific suction. Still we did not wish to jump before the place where we were standing would be only a few yards over the water, for we might be injured and not be able to swim.

We had no time to think now, only to act. We shook hands, wished each other luck. I said, 'Go ahead, I'll be right with you.' I threw my overcoat off as he climbed over the rail, sliding down facing the ship. Ten seconds later I sat on the rail. I faced out, and with a push of my arms and hands, jumped into the water as far out from the ship as I could. When we jumped we were only twelve or fifteen feet above the water. I never saw Long again. His body was later recovered. I am afraid that the few seconds elapsing between our going, meant the difference between being sucked into the deck below, as I believe he was, or pushed out by the backwash. I was pushed out and then sucked down.

The cold was terrific. The shock of the water took the breath out of my lungs. Down and down I went, spinning in all directions.

Swimming as hard as I could in the direction which I thought to be away from the ship, I finally came up with my lungs bursting, but not having taken any water. The ship was in front of me, 40 yards away. How long I had been swimming under water, I don't know. Perhaps a minute or less. Incidentally, my watch stopped at 2.22 am.

The story would not be complete without comment on the discipline and behaviour of the crew. They were perfect and did their full and complete duty. To see all the men covered with the dirt and grime of the boiler room, after having drawn the fires from the flooded stokehole, lined up on deck, awaiting orders, was a grand, inspiring sight. It was a tribute to the British Mercantile Marine.

Not a single engineering officer or engineer of the ship was saved. Every one was at his post in the engine room. They kept the lights going till the ship went under. They made the power for the CQD, which called for help through the night. Think what panic we might have had if the lights had failed; or worse yet, if the SS *Carpathia* had been unable to hear our call and learn our position.

Besides the full complement of engineers on the ship, headed by Chief Engineer William Bell, there were Archie Frost, Harland and Wolff's Chief Engineer, and about twenty assistants, together with Mr Thomas Andrews, one of the designers of the ship. Every single one died attending to his duty without a chance of being saved.

The ship seemed to be surrounded with a glare and stood out of the night as though she were on fire. I watched her. I don't know why I didn't keep swimming away. Fascinated, I seemed tied to the spot. Already I was tired out with the cold and struggling, although the life preserver held my head and shoulders above the water.

She continued to make the same forward progress as when I left her. The water was over the base of the first funnel. The mass of people on board were surging back, always back toward the floating stern. The rumble and roar continued, with even louder distinct wrenchings and tearings of boilers and engines from their beds. Suddenly the whole superstructure of the ship appeared to split, well forward to midship, and blow or buckle upwards. The second funnel, large enough for two automobiles to pass through abreast, seemed to be lifted off, emitting a cloud of sparks. It looked as if it would fall on top of me. It missed me by only twenty or thirty feet. The suction of it drew me down and down, struggling and swimming, practically spent.

As I finally came to the surface I put my hand over my head, in order to push away any obstruction. My hand came against something smooth and firm with rounded shape. I looked up, and realized that it was the cork fender of one of the collapsible lifeboats, which was floating in the water bottom side up. About four or five men were clinging to her bottom. I pulled myself up as far as I could, almost exhausted, but could not get my legs up. I asked them to give me a hand up, which they readily did. Sitting on my haunches and holding on for dear life, I was again facing the *Titanic*.

It seemed as though hours had passed since I left the ship; yet it was probably not more than four minutes, if that long. There was the gigantic mass, about 50 or 60 yards away. The forward motion had stopped. She was pivoting on a point just abaft of midship. Her stern was gradually rising into the air, seemingly in no hurry, just slowly and deliberately. The last funnel was about on the surface of the water. It was the dummy funnel, and I do not believe it fell.

Some months after the disaster, however, I had been invited to tell my story of the behaviour of the ship to the engineers and ship designers of the William Cramp and Sons' Ship and Engine Building Company, Richmond and Norris Streets, Philadelphia. I described the action in this way: the iceberg cut open about four of the *Titanic's* forward compartments, leaving, possibly, at least one buoyant compartment in the bow intact. With the buoyant stern tending to rise, and the bow tending slightly to do the same, the weight of the engines and boilers, which, torn from their beds, crashed in midship, possibly broke the keel downwards, and this in turn forced the superstructure to buckle or push up at the forward expansion joint; causing the funnel to fall. I did not say she broke into separate parts, but that some bending and breaking did take place. My hearers told me that it was a reasonable supposition and a possible explanation of the final behaviour of the ship.

Her deck was turned slightly toward us. We could see groups of the almost 1,500 people still aboard, clinging in clusters or bunches, like swarming bees; only to fall in masses, pairs or singly, as the great after part of the ship, 250 feet of it, rose into the sky, till it reached a 65 or 70 degree angle. Here it seemed to pause, and just hung, for what felt like minutes. Gradually she turned her deck away from us, as though to hide from our sight the awful spectacle.

We had an oar on our overturned boat. In spite of several men working it, amid our cries and prayers, we were being gradually sucked in toward the great pivoting mass. I looked upwards – we were right underneath the three enormous propellers. For an instant, I thought they were sure to come right down on top of us. Then, with the deadened noise of the bursting of her last few gallant bulkheads, she slid quietly away from us into the sea.

There was no final apparent suction, and practically no wreckage that we could see.

I don't remember all the wild talk and calls that were going on on our boat, but there was one concerted sigh or sob as she went from view.

Probably a minute passed with almost dead silence and quiet. Then an individual call for help, from here, from there; gradually swelling into a composite volume of one long continuous wailing chant, from the 1,500 in the water all around us. It sounded like locusts on a midsummer night, in the woods in Pennsylvania.

This terrible continuing cry lasted for twenty or thirty minutes, gradually dying away, as one after another could no longer withstand the cold and exposure. Practically no one was drowned, as no water was found in the lungs of those later recovered. Everyone had on a life preserver.

The partially filled lifeboats standing by, only a few hundred yards away never came back. Why on earth they did not come back is a mystery. How could any human being fail to heed those cries? They were afraid the boats would be swamped by people in the water.

The most heartrending part of the whole tragedy was the failure, right after the *Titanic* sank, of those boats which were only partially loaded, to pick up the poor souls in the water. There they were, only

400 or 500 yards away, listening to the cries, and still they did not come back. If they had turned back several hundred more would have been saved. No one can explain it. It was not satisfactorily explained in any investigation. It was just one of the many 'Acts of God' running through the whole disaster.

During this time, more and more were trying to get aboard the bottom of our overturned boat. We helped them on until we were packed like sardines. Then out of self-preservation, we had to turn some away. There were finally twenty-eight of us altogether on board. We were very low in the water. The water had roughened up slightly and was occasionally washing over us. The stars still shone brilliantly.

We were standing, sitting, kneeling, lying, in all conceivable positions, in order to get a small hold on the half inch overlap of the boat's planking, which was the only means of keeping ourselves from sliding off the slippery surface into that icy water. I was kneeling. A man was kneeling on my legs with his hands on my shoulders, and in turn somebody was on him. Once we obtained our original position we could not move. The assistant wireless man, Harold Bride, was lying across in front of me, with his legs in the water, and his feet jammed against the cork fender, which was about two feet under water.

We prayed and sang hymns. A great many of the men seemed to know each other intimately. Questions and answers were called around – who was on board, and who was lost, or what they had been seen doing? One call that came around was, 'Is the chief aboard?' Whether they meant Mr Wilde, the chief officer, or the chief engineer, or Captain Smith, I do not know. I do know that one of the circular life rings from the bridge was there when we got off in the morning. It may be that Captain Smith was on board with us for a while. Nobody knew where the 'Chief' was.

About twenty of our whole group were stokers. How they ever withstood the icy temperature after the heat they were accustomed to, is extraordinary, but there was no case of illness resulting. They surely were a grimy, wiry, dishevelled, hard looking lot. Under the surface they were brave human beings, with generous and charitable hearts.

Second Officer Lightoller, I discovered in the morning, was on board. He and some of the crew were trying to launch this boat before the *Titanic* sank. They were unsuccessful, but she floated off the deck covered with people, all of whom were shortly after washed off. Lightoller himself was washed off and sucked up against one of the ventilator grills. He had a terrific struggle, but finally again was able to reach the boat.

In August 1914, just as war declared, I sailed on the SS *Oceanic*, from New York, to play cricket in and around London, on a Merion Cricket Club team. Lightoller was either chief officer or first officer of the *Oceanic*, I am not certain which. We again went over our experiences and checked our ideas of just what had happened. We agreed on almost everything, with the exception of the splitting or bending of the ship. He did not think it broke at all.

Only four of us were passengers: Colonel Archibald Gracie, Washington, DC; A. H. Barkworth, East Riding, Yorkshire, England; W. J. Mellers, Chelsea, London, England; and myself.

Harold Bride helped greatly to keep our hopes up. He told us repeatedly which ships had answered his CQD (at that time the Morse code for help), and just how soon we might expect to sight them. He said time and time again, in answer to despairing doubters, 'The *Carpathia* is coming up as fast as she can. I gave her our position. There is no mistake. We should see her lights at about four or a little after.'

During all this time nobody dared to move, for we did not know at what moment our perilous support might overturn, throwing us all into the sea. The buoyant air was gradually leaking from under the boat, lowering us further and further into the water.

Sure enough, shortly before four o'clock we saw the masthead light of the *Carpathia* come over the horizon and creep toward us. We gave a thankful cheer. She came up slowly, oh, so slowly. Indeed she seemed to wait without getting any nearer. We thought hours and hours dragged by as she stood off in the distance. We had been trying all night to hail our other lifeboats. They did not hear us or would not answer. We knew they had plenty of room to take us aboard, if we could only make them realize our predicament. The *Carpathia*, waiting for a little more light, was slowly coming up on the boats and was picking them up. With the dawn breaking, we could see them being hoisted from the water. For us, afraid we might overturn any minute, the suspense was terrible.

The long-hoped-for dawn actually broke, and with it a breeze came up, making our raft rock more and more. The air under us escaped at a more rapid rate, lowering us still further into the water. We had visions of sinking before the help so near at hand could reach us.

With daylight we could see what we were doing and took courage to move, stretch and untangle ourselves.

One by one those on top of the freezing group stood up, until all of us who could stand were on our feet, with the exception of poor Bride, who could not bear his weight on his, but could only pull his feet and legs slightly out of the water. The waves washed over the upturned bottom more and more, as we sank lower and the water became rougher. To keep our buoyancy, we tried to offset the roll by leaning all together first to one side and then to the other.

About 6.30, after continued and desperate calling, we attracted the attention of the other lifeboats. Two of them finally realized the position we were in and drew toward us. Lightoller had found his whistle, and more because of it than our hoarse shouts, their attention was attracted.

It took them ages to cover the three or four hundred yards between us. As they approached, we could see that so few men were in them that some of the oars were being pulled by women. In neither of them was much room for extra passengers, for they were two of the very few boats to be loaded to near capacity. The first took off half of us. My mother was in this boat, having rowed most of the night. She says she thought she recognized me. I did not see her. The other boat took aboard the rest of us. We had to lift Harold Bride. He was in a bad way and, I think, would have slipped off the bottom of our overturned boat, if several of us had not held onto him for the last half hour.

It was just about this time that the edge of the sun came above the horizon. Then, to feel its glowing warmth, which we had never expected to see again, was something, never to be forgotten. Even through my numbness I began to realize that I was saved – that I would live.

The *Carpathia* was about eight hundred yards away, picking up the people from one boat after another as fast as she could. Gradually we drew alongside of her. There was a rope ladder with wooden steps hanging down her side. Most of us climbed up it, although many had to be hauled up in slings or chairs. It was now almost 7.30 am We were the last boat to be gathered in. The only signs of ice were four small, very scattered bergs, way off in the distance.

As I reached the top of the ladder, I suddenly

saw my mother. When she saw me, she thought, of course, that my father must be with me. She was overjoyed to see me, but it was a terrible shock to hear that I had not seen father since he had said goodbye to her.

As we talked, somebody gave me a coffee cup full of brandy. It was the first drink of an alcoholic beverage I had ever had. It warmed me as though I had put hot coals in my stomach, and did more too. A man kindly loaned me his pyjamas and his bunk, then my wet clothes were taken to be dried, and with the help of the brandy I went to sleep till almost noon. I got up feeling fit and well, just as though nothing bad had happened. After putting on my own clothes, which were entirely dry, I hurried out to look for mother. We were then passing to the south of a solid ice field, which I was told was over twenty miles long and four miles wide.

I found that Captain Arthur H. Rostron, Commander of the *Carpathia*, of the Cunard Line, had given up his cabin to my mother, Mrs George D. Widener, and Mrs John Jacob Astor. I slept on the floor of the cabin every night until we reached New York on Thursday evening, April 18th.

The passengers and crew of the *Carpathia* were wonderfully good to us, looking to our every need and comfort. Enough cannot be said to describe the bravery of Captain Rostron, in his taking the tremendous responsibility of running through that dense ice field, full speed ahead, to our rescue.

The trip back to New York was one big heartache

and misery. There were 705 survivors on board, 1503 having been lost. It seemed as if there were none but widows left, each one mourning the loss of her husband. It was a most pitiful sight. All were hoping beyond hope, even for weeks afterwards, that some ship, somehow, had picked up their loved one, and that he would be eventually among the saved.

Because I had known Ismay so well on board the *Titanic*, the doctor of the *Carpathia*, the afternoon that we approached New York, asked me if I would visit Mr Ismay in his cabin and talk to him, to see if I could not help relieve the terribly nervous condition he was in.

I immediately went down and as there was no answer to my knock, I went right in. He was seated, in his pyjamas, on his bunk, staring straight ahead, shaking all over like a leaf.

My entrance apparently did not dawn on his consciousness. Even when I spoke to him and tried to engage him in conversation, telling him that he had a perfect right to take the last boat, he paid absolutely no attention and continued to look ahead with his fixed stare.

I am almost certain that on the *Titanic* his hair had been black with slight tinges of gray, but now his hair was virtually snow white.

I have never seen a man so completely wrecked. Nothing I could do or say brought any response.

As I closed the door, he was still looking fixedly ahead.

The final docking in New York at Pier No. 54 North River, when all our friends and relations learned the truth about the extent of the loss, was the last nerve-shattering blow for many people. For those who were ashore, it marked the end of all hope. With the exception of lawsuits and investigations, it was the closing chapter of the greatest and most distressing disaster of the sea the world has yet seen.

BONUS MATERIAL: JACK THAYER'S OTHER PUBLISHED ACCOUNTS

1. Account included in Logan Marshall's edited book 'Sinking of the Titanic and Great Sea Disasters', published in 1912

This book was the first anthology of survivor accounts. Logan was a journalist and produced a cut and paste 'instant book' that was hawked across America sold door to door in the months following the disaster in 1912.

Chapter XV Jack Thayer's Own Story of the Wreck

Seventeen-year-old son of Pennsylvania railroad official tells moving story of his rescue – told mother to be brave – separated from parents – jumped when vessel sank – drifted on overturned boat picked up by *Carpathia*

One of the calmest of the passengers was young Jack Thayer, the seventeen-year-old son of Mr and Mrs John B. Thayer. When his mother was put into the lifeboat he kissed her and told her to be brave, saying that he and his father would be all right. He and Mr Thayer stood on the deck as the small boat in which Mrs Thayer was a passenger made off from the side of the *Titanic* over the smooth sea.

The boy's own account of his experience as told to one of his rescuers is one of the most remarkable of all the wonderful ones that have come from the tremendous catastrophe:

'Father was in bed, and mother and myself were about to get into bed. There was no great shock, I was on my feet at the time and I do not think it was enough to throw anyone down. I put on an overcoat and rushed up on 'A' deck on the port side. I saw nothing there. I then went forward to the bow to see if I could see any signs of ice. The only ice I saw was on the well deck. I could not see very far ahead, having just come out of a brightly lighted room.

I then went down to our room and my father and mother came on deck with me, to the starboard side of 'A' deck. We could not see anything there. Father thought he saw small pieces of ice floating around, but I could not see any myself. There was no big berg. We walked around to the port side, and the ship had then a fair list to port. We stayed there looking over the side for about five minutes. The list seemed very slowly to be increasing.

We then went down to our rooms on 'C' deck, all

of us dressing quickly, putting on all our clothes. We all put on life-preservers, and over these we put our overcoats. Then we hurried up on deck and walked around, looking out at different places until the women were all ordered to collect on the port side.'

SEPARATED FROM PARENTS

'Father and I said goodbye to mother at the top of the stairs on 'A' deck. She and the maid went right out on 'A' deck on the port side and we went to the starboard side. As at this time we had no idea the boat would sink we walked around 'A' deck and then went to 'B' deck. Then we thought we would go back to see if mother had gotten off safely, and went to the port side of 'A' deck. We met the chief steward of the main dining saloon and he told us that mother had not yet taken a boat, and he took us to her.

Father and mother went ahead and I followed. They went down to 'B' deck and a crowd got in front of me and I was not able to catch them, and lost sight of them. As soon as I could get through the crowd I tried to find them on 'B' deck, but without success. That is the last time I saw my father. This was about one half an hour before she sank. I then went to the starboard side, thinking that father and mother must have gotten off in a boat. All of this time I was with a fellow named Milton C. Long, of New York, whom I had just met that evening.

On the starboard side the boats were getting away quickly. Some boats were already off in a distance. We thought of getting into one of the boats, the last boat to go on the forward part of the starboard side, but there seemed to be such a crowd around I thought it unwise to make any attempt to get into it. He and I stood by the davits of one of the boats that had left. I did not notice anybody that I knew except Mr Lindley, whom I had also just met that evening. I lost sight of him in a few minutes. Long and I then stood by the rail just a little aft of the captain's bridge.'

THOUGHT SHIP WOULD FLOAT

'The list to the port had been growing greater all the time. About this time the people began jumping from the stern. I thought of jumping myself, but was afraid of being stunned on hitting the water. Three times I made up my mind to jump out and slide down the davit ropes and try to make the boats that were lying off from the ship, but each time Long got hold of me and told me to wait a while. He then sat down and I stood up waiting to see what would happen. Even then we thought she might possibly stay afloat.

I got a sight on a rope between the davits and a star and noticed that she was gradually sinking. About this time she straightened up on an even keel and started to go down fairly fast at an angle of about 30 degrees. As she started to sink we left the davits and went back and stood by the rail about even with the second funnel.

Long and myself said goodbye to each other and jumped up on the rail. He put his legs over and held on a minute and asked me if I was coming. I told him I would be with him in a minute. He did not jump clear, but slid down the side of the ship. I never saw him again.

About five seconds after he jumped I jumped out, feet first. I was clear of the ship; went down, and as I came up I was pushed away from the ship by some force. I came up facing the ship, and one of the funnels seemed to be lifted off and fell towards me about 15 yards away, with a mass of sparks and steam coming out of it. I saw the ship in a sort of a red glare, and it seemed to me that she broke in two just in front of the third funnel.

This time I was sucked down, and as I came up I was pushed out again and twisted around by a large wave, coming up in the midst of a great deal of small wreckage. As I pushed my hand from my head it touched the cork fender of an over-turned lifeboat. I looked up and saw some men on the top and asked them to give me a hand. One of them, who was a stoker, helped me up. In a short time the bottom was covered with about twenty-five or thirty men. When I got on this I was facing the ship.'

SKETCHES OF THE TITANIC BY 'JACK' THAYER

These sketches were outlined by John B. Thayer, Jr, on the day of the disaster, and afterwards filled in by L. D. Skidmon [sic], of Brooklyn. [See illustrations 2-7 reproduced earlier in this book]

'The stern then seemed to rise in the air and stopped at about an angle of 60 degrees. It seemed to hold there for a time and then with a hissing sound it shot right down out of sight with people jumping from the stern. The stern either pivoted around towards our boat, or we were sucked towards it, and as we only had one oar we could not keep away. There did not seem to be very much suction and most of us managed to stay on the bottom of our boat.

We were then right in the midst of fairly large wreckage, with people swimming all around us. The sea was very calm and we kept the boat pretty steady, but every now and then a wave would wash over it.'

SAID THE LORD'S PRAYER

'The assistant wireless operator was right next to me, holding on to me and kneeling in the water. We all sang a hymn and said the Lord's Prayer, and then waited for dawn to come. As often as we saw the other boats in a distance we would yell, 'Ship ahoy!' But they could not distinguish our cries from any of the others, so we all gave it up, thinking it useless. It was very cold and none of us were able to move around to keep warm, the water washing over her almost all the time.

Toward dawn the wind sprang up, roughening up the water and making it difficult to keep the boat balanced. The wireless man raised our hopes a great deal by telling us that the *Carpathia* would be up in about three hours. About 3.30 or 4 o'clock some men on our boat on the bow sighted her mast lights. I could not see them, as I was sitting down with a man kneeling on my leg. He finally got up and I stood up. We had the second officer, Mr Lightoller, on board. We had an officer's whistle and whistled for the boats in the distance to come up and take us off.

It took about an hour and a half for the boats to draw near. Two boats came up. The first took half and the other took the balance, including myself. We had great difficulty about this time in balancing the boat, as the men would lean too far, but we were all taken aboard the already crowded boat, and in about a half or three-quarters of an hour later we were picked up by the *Carpathia*.

I have noticed Second Officer Lightoller's statement that "J. B. Thayer was on our overturned boat," which would give the impression that it was father, when he really meant it was I, as he only learned my name in a subsequent conversation on the *Carpathia*, and did not know I was "junior."'

2. Accounts pieced together by Archibald Gracie in his book, 'The Truth About the Titanic', published in 1913
Archibald Gracie was a fellow survivor and had had a very similar escape from the sinking *Titanic* to that of Jack, both swimming to the upturned lifeboat, collapsible B.

Gracie: The experience of my fellow passenger on this boat, John 'Jack' B. Thayer, is embodied in accounts written by him on 20 and 23 April and, just after landing from the *Carpathia*: the first given to the press as the only statement he had made, the second in a very pathetic letter written to Judge Charles L. Long, of Springfield, Massachusetts, whose son, Milton C. Long, was a companion of young Thayer all that evening, 14 April until at the very last both jumped into the sea and Long was lost, as described:

'Thinking that father and mother had managed to get off in a boat we, Long and myself, went to the starboard side of the boat deck where the boats were getting away quickly. Some were already off in the distance. We thought of getting into one of them, the last boat on the forward part of the starboard side, but there seemed to be such a crowd around that I thought it unwise to make any attempt to get into it. I thought it would never reach the water right side up, but it did.

Here I noticed nobody that I knew except Mr Lingrey, whom I had met for the first time that evening. I lost sight of him in a few minutes. Long and I then stood by the rail just a little aft of the captain's bridge. There was such a big list to port that it seemed as if the ship would turn on her side.

About this time the people began jumping from the stern. I thought of jumping myself, but was afraid of being stunned on hitting the water. Three times I made up my mind to jump out and slide down the davit ropes and try to swim to the boats that were lying off from the ship, but each time Long got hold of me and told me to wait a while. I got a sight on a rope between the davits and a star and noticed that the ship was gradually sinking. About this time she straightened up on an even keel again, and started to go down fairly fast at an angle of about 30 degrees. As she started to sink we left the davits and went back and stood by the rail aft, even with the second funnel. Long and myself stood by each other and jumped on the rail. We did not give each other any messages for home because neither of us thought we would ever get back. Long put his legs over the rail, while I straddled it. Hanging over the side and holding on to the rail with his hands he looked up at me and said: 'You are coming, boy, aren't you?' I replied: 'Go ahead I'll be with you in a minute.' He let go and slid down the side and I never saw him again. Almost immediately after he jumped I jumped. All this last part took a very short time, and when we jumped we were about 10 yards above the water. Long was perfectly calm all the time and kept his nerve to the very end.'

Gracie: How he sank and finally reached the upturned boat is quoted accurately from the newspaper report from this same source given in my personal narrative. 17-year-old 'Jack' Thayer was also on the starboard side of the ship, and jumped from the rail before the Engelhardt boat was swept from the boat deck by the 'giant wave.' Young Thayer's reported description of this is as follows:

'I jumped out, feet first, went down, and as I came up I was pushed away from the ship by some force. I was sucked down again, and as I came up I was pushed out again and twisted around by a large wave, coming up in the midst of a great deal of small wreckage. My hand touched the canvas fender of an overturned lifeboat. I looked up and saw some men on the top. One of them helped me up. In a short time the bottom was covered with 25 or 30 men. The assistant wireless operator (Bride) was right next to me holding on to me and kneeling in the water.'

Gracie: He continues as follows:

'As often as we saw other boats in the distance we would yell, 'Ship ahoy!' but they could not distinguish our cries from any of the others, so we all gave it up, thinking it useless. It was very cold, and the water washed over the upset boat almost all the time. Towards dawn the wind sprung up, roughening the water and making it difficult to keep the boat balanced. The wireless man raised our hopes a great deal by telling us that the *Carpathia* would be up in about three hours. About 3.30 am or four o'clock some men at the bow of our boat sighted her mast lights. I could not see them as I was sitting down with a man kneeling on my leg. He finally got up, and I stood up. We had the Second Officer, Mr Lightoller, on board. He had an officer's whistle and whistled for the boats in the distance to come up and take us off. Two of them came up. The first took half and the other took the balance, including myself. In the transfer we had difficulty in balancing our boat as the men would lean too far over, but we were all taken aboard the already crowded boats and taken to the *Carpathia* in safety.'

LIST OF
ILLUSTRATIONS

1. 1912 photograph of collapsible lifeboat B that Jack Thayer was saved by, discovered adrift in the Atlantic by crew from *Mackay-Bennett* the ship sent to recover bodies of the *Titanic's* victims. Spitfire Publishers Image Collection.

2. *Titanic* strikes the iceberg 11.45 p.m. First in a series of six sketches drawn on board *Carpathia* on 15 April by Lewis Skidmore (a young art teacher), based on conversations with Jack Thayer following his rescue. The sketches were first published in American newspapers in 1912 and by 1940 when Jack published this book some of the timings attributed to the drawings were proved a little inaccurate. Spitfire Publishers Image Collection 2195b98p201TL.

3. '*Titanic* settles by head, boats ordered out.' Spitfire Publishers Image Collection 2196b98p201ML.

4. '*Titanic* settles to forward stack, breaks between stacks'. Jack is one of only a handful of survivors to describe the ship breaking in two as she sank. Many survivors refuted this assessment but seventy

years later Jack and others was proved right when the wreck was discovered resting on the seabed in two halves. Spitfire Publishers Image Collection 2197b98p201BL.

5. '*Titanic's* forward end floats then sinks'. Spitfire Publishers Image Collection 2198b98p201TR.

6. 'Stern section of *Titanic* pivots and swings over spot where forward section sank'. Spitfire Publishers Image Collection 2199b98p201MR.

7. Final position in which Titanic stayed for several minutes before the final plunge'. Spitfire Publishers Image Collection 2200b98p201BR.